It's a Jungle Out There

Peter Millett
Richard Morden

Australia • Brazil • Japan • Korea • Mexico • Singapore • Spain • United Kingdom • United States

It's a Jungle Out There

Fast Forward
Silver Level 23

Text: Peter Millett
Illustrations: Richard Morden
Editor: Johanna Rohan
Design: Mandi Cole
Series design: James Lowe
Production controller: Seona Galbally
Audio recordings: Juliet Hill, Picture Start
Spoken by: Matthew King and Abbe Holmes
Reprint: Siew Han Ong

ISBN 978 0 17 012695 3
ISBN 978 0 17 012693 9 (set)

Cengage Learning Australia
Level 7, 80 Dorcas Street
South Melbourne, Victoria Australia 3205
Phone: 1300 790 853

Cengage Learning New Zealand
Unit 4B Rosedale Office Park
331 Rosedale Road, Albany, North Shore NZ 0632
Phone: 0508 635 766

For learning solutions, visit cengage.com.au

Printed in Australia by Ligare Pty Ltd
6 7 8 9 10 11 20 19 18 17 16

Evaluated in independent research by staff from the Department of Language, Literacy and Arts Education at the University of Melbourne.

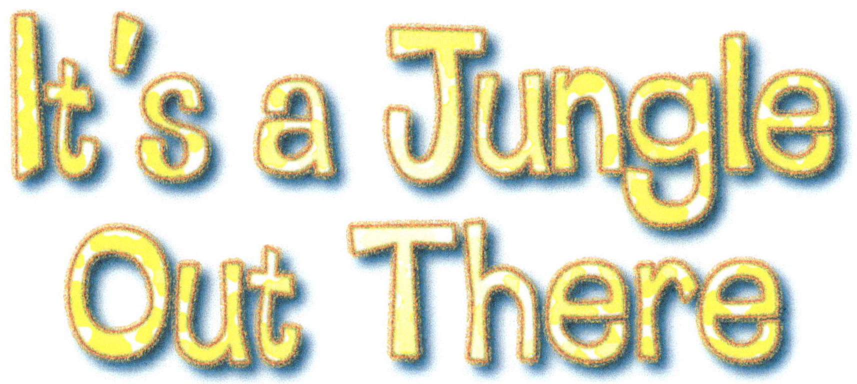

It's a Jungle Out There

Peter Millett
Richard Morden

Contents

Meet Thomas Wilson

Meet Thomas Wilson.
Thomas is famous all over the world.
He holds the world record
for sleeping in.
One weekend, Thomas slept in for
two days, three hours
and fourteen minutes.
It was unbelievable.
No one in history had ever slept in
for so long before.

Thomas was very proud of his world record.
His friends were proud of him, too.
Whenever Thomas walked down the street, people always came up to him and shook his hand.
Thomas was a star.

The only person who wasn't proud
of Thomas's world record
was his father.

Dad didn't like it when Thomas slept in.
He complained that whenever
Thomas slept in
the lawns didn't get mowed.
He was worried about how high
the grass was getting.
Every weekend, it seemed to get
higher and higher.
"It's like a jungle out there,"
Dad moaned to Thomas one day.

But Thomas wasn't worried about the grass getting higher.

He had more important things on his mind – like sleeping in.

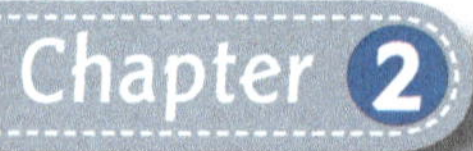

What on Earth ...?

One morning, Thomas was woken
from a deep sleep
by a loud roaring noise.
It sounded like a wild animal
pacing about under his
bedroom window.
Thomas rushed over to the window
and pulled the curtains back.
His eyes bulged like basketballs.
"What on Earth *...?*" he gasped.

There, in the middle of the backyard,
was a lion!
"Awesome!" cried Thomas.

Running Words 226

Suddenly, a giraffe poked its head through the window.
It munched the leaves from a plant sitting by Thomas's bed.
Next, Thomas saw an elephant walk past the swimming pool and squirt water all over Dad's car.
"Cool!" cheered Thomas.
"Now I don't have to wash Dad's car today."

Thomas grabbed his camera
and sprinted down the stairs.
"Dad, Dad, you were right!"
he shouted.
"The backyard has turned into a jungle.
Come and see! It's amazing!"
Thomas rushed outside and started
taking photos of the animals.

Dad poked his head outside to see what all the commotion was.
"Oh, my!" he cried, spilling his coffee as a rhinoceros ran past him.
"No, no ... this can't be happening," he cried.
"It's a disaster!"

"Don't worry, Dad," said Thomas.
"It's only spilled coffee.
We can clean it up later."

"Thomas, this is your fault. If you had mowed the lawns, we wouldn't be stuck in the middle of a jungle!" Dad shouted.

Thomas shrugged his shoulders. "Actually, Dad, I think it's really cool. Think of all the money we'll save on trips to the zoo."

Thomas's father stormed off,
while Thomas got
a group of chimpanzees
to pose for a photo.

Then, he e-mailed the photo to the
local newspaper.
Five minutes later the phone rang.
"Yes, that's right –
a lion, a giraffe, an elephant, a rhinoceros
and some chimpanzees,"
Thomas said to the shocked reporter.

Chapter 3

The Amazing Backyard Jungle

By lunchtime, the skies above Thomas's house were buzzing with helicopters.
People filled the streets, queuing up to see the animals.

Thomas stood outside holding a large sign above his head.
"Roll up, roll up, get your tickets here," he bellowed.
"Be the first to join my amazing backyard jungle tour!"

Suddenly, the crowd rushed towards Thomas.
"I want to be first!"

"No, I want to be first!"

The people pushed and shoved each other to get to the front of the queue.
Thomas charged ten dollars for adults, five dollars for children, and seven dollars for students.
He also gave away free posters of himself to the first ten people who bought tickets.

The tour was a huge hit.
People came from all over the city
to see it.
The crowds 'oh'd' and 'ah'd'
as they watched the magnificent lions
sunning themselves on the patio,
the graceful giraffes chewing
on the petunias,
and the playful chimpanzees
performing tricks on Thomas's
new skateboard.

In less than five minutes,
Thomas made more money
from his tour than he had made
all year working at PT's Burger Palace.
He felt very proud of himself.
So did his father.
"Thomas, I've got to hand it to you –
you sure are a smart kid," Dad smiled.

When the crowds went home,
Thomas counted all the money
he had made.
He decided to buy something special
to celebrate his fantastic success.
He raced out and bought his dad
a super deluxe ride-on lawnmower.

"Here you go, Dad, this is for you,"
he said excitedly.

"For me?" asked Dad.

"Yes, Dad, for you!"

Dad jumped on his new ride-on
lawn mower and happily started mowing
the lawns.

Thomas then slumped back
in his hammock
and quietly sipped an ice-cold drink
in the warm afternoon sun.
"Ah, this is the life," he smiled,
drifting off into a deep sleep.

Chapter 4

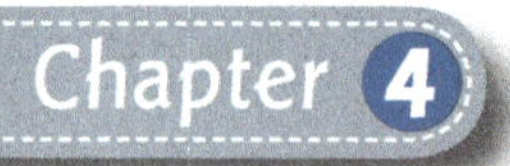

The Noisy Old Lawnmower

Suddenly, Thomas was woken from
his peaceful sleep
by a loud roaring noise.
He looked down and shivered
with shock.
He wasn't lying in a hammock –
he was lying in his bed!
"What the?!" he cried.

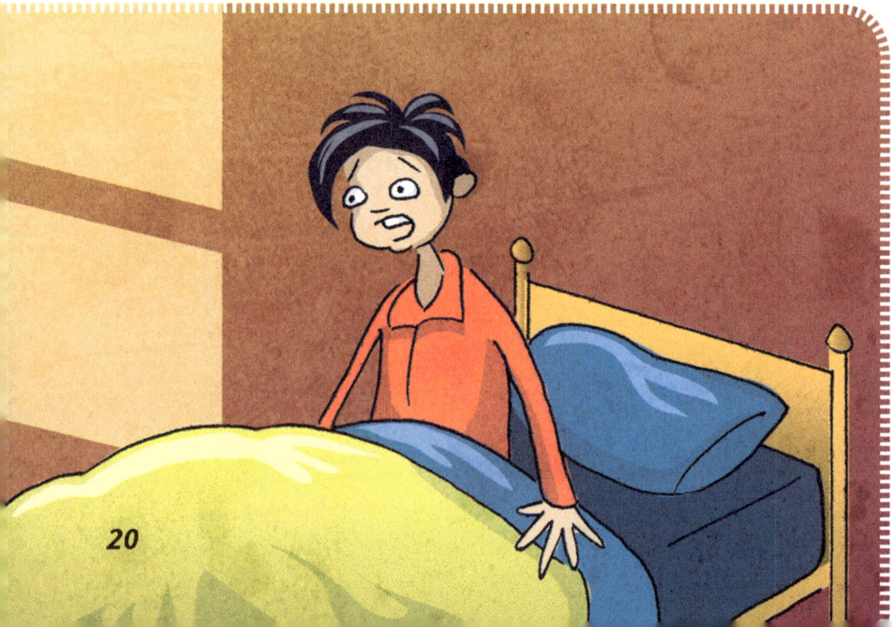

Thomas pulled back the curtains.
He stared out into the backyard.
His face turned white.
There were no animals anywhere –
no giggling chimpanzees,
no yawning lions,
no hungry giraffes –
just row after row of unmown grass.
"Oh, no," he groaned.
"I must have dreamed
the whole thing!"

Thomas looked to his left
and saw his father standing over
a noisy old lawnmower
blowing thick black smoke
all over the backyard.

"Hey, Thomas," cried Dad.
"I finally managed to get this noisy old lawnmower going –
how about you come down
and help me mow the lawns?"

Thomas smiled painfully at his father
and waved.

Thomas realised that the lawns
needed mowing,
the car needed washing,
and who knows how many other jobs
still needed doing.
So, he decided there was only one
place for him to be – back in bed.

He jumped into his bed
and pulled the covers over his head.
"Ah," he said, grinning.
"It's time I set a new world record!"